Watching Wisteria

by Duane Locke

Vida Publishing
Baltimore • Orlando

Permission acknowledgments appear on page ix.

Hardcover and soft cover editions of this book published simultaneously in 1995 by Vida Publishing, Inc.

Watching Wisteria Copyright © 1995 by Duane Locke. All rights reserved. Printed in the United States of America. No part of this book may be used or reproduced in any manner whatsoever without written permission except in the case of brief quotations embodied in critical articles and reviews. For information address Vida Publishing, Inc., P.O. Box 296, Glyndon, MD 21071.

Cover photograph by Sam Pathi

Design and production by Great Impressions Design, Inc., Bel Air, MD 21014

Library of Congress preassigned card number: 95-60912

Locke, Duane, 1921-
Watching Wisteria: poems / Duane Locke.

I. Title
811'.54
ISBN: 0-9632547-4-X (cloth)
ISBN: 0-9632547-5-8 (paper)
First Edition

For
Paul B. Roth and Alan Britt

CONTENTS

Introduction 3
Roman Summer 9
Childhood Impression, Tampa 12
Trestle 13
Post Office 14
White Tree by the Gulf 17
Ludwig II 18
Winter 21
An Edwardian Lady 23
Life Imitates Art 28
The Camera Di Psiche, Palazzo Del Te, Mantova 30
Eleonora of Toledo 32
Edict of Milan, Circa 300 AD 34
Vienna Woods, 1903 36
A Composer for Prepared Piano
   Writes to a Representational Painter 39
An Employee of the Bureau of Gerontology 41
The Dwarf 45
With Byron at Diodati 46
An Umbrella Leaf 48
An Abandoned Warehouse at Cedar Key 49
Venus and Adonis 50
Venus 51
The Repaired Venus 52
Out in a Pasture 53
The End of Something 54
Fences 56
A Return to the 'Eighties 57
A Philosopher Eating a Lobster 58

CONTENTS continued

Love in the 'Eighties 59
A Neoteric, the Nemesis 60
Repainted for Quick Sale 61
Tanagers 62
Jan Vermeer, the Artist in His Studio,
    Vienna Kuntsthistorishches Museum 63
Chinese Yu Vessel 64
A Kingfisher Over a North Carolina River 65
New Altars 66
The People and the Terrorist 67
Migrations and Myths 68
Procession in Pisa 69
Contrasts 70
Class Reunion 71

viii

ACKNOWLEDGMENTS

Grateful acknowledgments are made to the editors of the following magazines in which these poems were published:

Artsnews: "An Umbrella Leaf"

Abraxas: "The Camera Di Psiche, Palazzo Del Te, Montova"

American Poetry Review: "Roman Summer," "Childhood Impression, Tampa," "Trestle," "Post Office," and "White Tree by the Gulf"

Black Moon: "Jan Vermeer, Artist in his Studio," and "The People and the Terrorist"

Bogg: "With Byron at Diodati"

Cape Rock Quarterly: "The Dwarf"

Confrontation: "Eleonora of Toledo"

DeKalb Literary Journal: "Edict of Milan, Circa 300 AD"

The Literary Review: "Ludwig II," "Winter," "An Edwardian Lady," and "Life Imitates Art"

Midwest Quarterly: "Venus," "Repaired Venus," "Out in a Pasture," "End of Something," "Fences," "A Return to the 'Eighties," "A Philosopher Eating a Lobster," "Love in the 'Eighties," "A Neoteric, The Nemesis," and "Repainted for Quick Sale"

Negative Capability: "Vienna Woods, 1903," "A Composer for Prepared Piano Writes to a Representational Painter," and "An Employee of the Bureau of Gerontology"

Tampa Tribune: "An Abandoned Warehouse at Cedar Key" and "Venus and Adonis"

INTRODUCTION

Duane Locke and the Immoral Tradition
by Fred Chappell

The publication of *Watching Wisteria* ought to mark an important point, if not indeed a turning point, in the career of Duane Locke. But I do not think that this poet, who is one of the most fascinating of our contemporaries, will regard it as such; I do not believe that Locke thinks in these terms. Here is a poet, after all, who has published more than 1500 poems in more than 500 periodicals, as well as 14 chapbooks. He could have chosen long ago to bring out a Selected or even a Collected Poems.

That he has not done so is a fact that helps to characterize his stance, one which I shall describe as a supreme skepticism, a knowing unwillingness to put easy faith in such notions as *turning points of poetic careers, noblest achievements of human spirit, profound revelations of psychic darkness*, and so forth. His poetic ideals will include, I feel, little reverence for the monumental, the self-important, the official.

Locke writes many persona poems, so it is not always accurate to impute the sentiments of his stanzas personally to him, but I suspect that four lines from "An Abandoned Warehouse at Cedar Key" express an idea he finds congenial: "I think Tennyson would have been a better poet / if he had stuck to rusted nails, / fallen rose leaves, shattered spars, / and forgot about the Holy Grail." Other poets have agreed with this thought (most famously, perhaps, W. H. Auden), but few of them are willing to accept as goals for poetry such modest ones as Locke accepts.

It is not that his poems lack ambition; indeed, they are products of severe intellectual and emotional engagement. But the poet's allegiances are to the subject at hand, to its expression in new, and even novel, artistic furnishing. This expression is fleet, alert, savvy, debonair, and sometimes seemingly improvisational; a philosophy underpins it but knowledge of that philosophy on the part of the reader is not necessary for the enjoyment of the expression itself.

Which is to say—in rather a roundabout way—that while Duane Locke may be skeptical of the pretended glories of art, he is never condescending; he gives his readers the best he has got. He only does not desire to make grandiose claims for what he offers. This attitude is more than personal diffidence; it is one of his poetic tenets, one that gives us an impression of the attention behind these poems that pause in midflight to take in their topics the way that butterflies stop off at certain abelia blossoms while pursuing travels that an observer finds beautiful but bewildering in their total design.

The speaker of "Roman Summer" articulates this attitude: "Then I flipped a coin, / accepted its advice / to become respectable / and lost." The ironies are casual, but multifoliate and telling; the speaker has decided to become "respectable" by tossing a coin, accepting the fact that in his own view "respectable" means "lost." It is an act of rebellion, this cointoss; it necessitates the entire making-over of a personality that had become burdensome because it had become false: "As I survey my errors, / I realize that I spent / too much time in graveyards / conversing with my ancestors, / beseeching, begging / the whereabouts of what is called 'the real world.'"

I have the feeling sometimes that Locke might ring out the Voltairean war-whoop, "Escrasez l'infame," while charging in full attack not upon established religion but upon established art, established ideas. I would wager that to some degree at least he identifies himself with the speaker in "A Composer for Prepared Piano Writes to a Representational Painter": "You must change your style of painting, / it is immoral to paint traditionally." The poet could agree too with his persona's rationale: "I love the earth too much / to continue to compose / according to the tradition of old." Where he would disagree with the speaker (and it is one of the poem's best ironies that he does disagree) is in the estimation of the importance of his art: "With a new art, the prepared piano, / I might transform people and create a decent society."

I would not be surprised to learn that Duane Locke has tested most new schools of art and thought, has considered and enjoyed them, and then has gone on to something even newer or has rediscovered an older way of thinking and writing. He was once, he claims, "a pre-premodern" and has now become "a post-postmodern," and I do not doubt this claim. Any poet who has been for such a long time such a devoted thinker and reader will often find that he has anticipated certain philosophic fashions and has already discounted others—while never receiving credit for his discoveries, anticipations, and rebuttals. It is one of the most luscious paradoxes of our time that theorists cannot allow themselves to imagine that writers are able to think philosophically while at the same time piling up thousands of subtle pages about the works of these figures they regard as non-thinkers.

A poet like Locke will be the despair of doctrinaire theoreticians. It is clear from his poems that he has pondered deeply the theoretical tendencies of his art ("Direction has blunted perception; / what is familiar must be doctored / before it can…become actual," says his Composer), yet he has not tendered allegiance to any brand of theory or school of philosophy. He has felt within himself the movement of the currents of modern thought and feeling, but he has not joined any group large or small. He believes, I expect, that the only sort of thought that is genuine is that which is independent, that the only poet who understands others is the one who stands alone. That is why I take "White Tree by the Gulf" as a self-portrait. It is not self-vaunting, neither is it self-pitying, but it comes out sounding more traditionally romantic than most of Duane Locke's other poems. That fact too is an ironic paradox, for the lines embody a determined attempt at objective accuracy:

> My life is lived by
> a white, barkless shoreline tree
> that stands with a dark hole

for a bright woodpecker beside the gulf.
I have stood in the distance
where mangroves arch over
the horseshoe crabs' backs
to watch the rainbowed foam
flow over the white roots.
The distant foam flows inside my body,
its salt my heart's blood,
the woodpecker's peck my heart beat.

Fred Chappell is a poet, fiction writer and critic who teaches English at the University of North Carolina at Greensboro. His latest book is *Spring Garden: New and Selected Poems* from Louisiana State University Press.

WATCHING WISTERIA

ROMAN SUMMER

I sit, this summer, watching wisteria,
spin, settle pale purple by my small white cup.
This morning, the fat, bald proprietor
who like a jailer keeps keys dangling from his belt,
brought amaretto as a corrective for espresso.
The albergo dog who lives behind a "Attenti Carne" sign
wears my green striped shorts.
My laundry fell from a window ledge used as a clothesline
into this dog's private world.
Seeing his teeth, hearing his snarl,
I surrendered the rights to my property,
as I always have.

For some time, I have been writing *la vita altra* poems,
trying to discover my identity
through someone who lived in the fourteenth century;
but now I have adopted the *donna lontana* genre.
My models are Dante, Petrarch, Montale and the mynah bird
who recites from a cage in the hall.
The bird calls every woman Beatrice, Laura and Clizia.

Today, I am a victim of my politeness and courtesy,
having responded to a letter
from a person I hardly knew
when we were close friends,
as colleagues in the humanities at an egregious university.
I promised to serve as the guide he could not afford.
He has a penchant for the baroque,
and desires a sexual liaison with Saint Teresa.

As I wait and write another long letter
that will not be read or will be quickly tossed
into a pile of memorabilia,
random thoughts drift through my mind:
Michelangelo reported that the waters
of Lombardy gave the cats goiters;
a line out of Bonnefoy:

ainsi je t'inventais parmi tes cheveux clairs;
the orange and grey bird that hopped
behind your blonde hair
as you entered at Bomarzo
a lopsided house in the garden of monstrosities.

I fidget, trying to remove
from my neck with the loose old skin an invisible collar
with its leash
held by the hand of habit,
a hand whose king sized fingernails
are artificial, glued on, and rose red.
I have been walked
as a pet dog
around the park
too many winters.

Once I was a timid nomad,
sleeping alone by rain puddles
standing in an evacuation,
surrounded by trees
that looked like cloths unraveling,
a feeble fire in a bent wash tub,
my companion an owl.
Then I flipped a coin,
accepted its advice
to become respectable
and lost.

I see this reputed expert on Hemingway
crossing the street.
He stops in the middle and I read on his lips,
"Dové Albergo Pavia?"
Now, he is walking
through the section
where gays meet
and make propositions,

now turning down a tree shadowed sidewalk
by the fence outside the Baths of Diocletian
where the buses park and wait
to go to Tivoli and the Villa d'Este.
This pathway is primarily used as a urinal.

Old men living on their Italian pensions,
dressed formally and neat, walk
to get in line around the corner
where in a theatre a girl from Tampa, Florida
who dyed her brown hair blonde
will do at two, four, six, eight, and ten
a strip tease.

My electrocardiograph says I am immortal,
immortal physically, but everything spiritual
that I have done is already dead.

As I survey my errors,
I realize that I spent
too much time in graveyards
conversing with my ancestors,
beseeching, begging
the whereabouts of what is called "the real world".

They answered in a chorus,
their many voices
blended into pure sound.
One soloist, a high soprano,
sent her ghost to the proscenium
and did a vocalise.

CHILDHOOD IMPRESSION, TAMPA

The journey, questless, the holy grail folded
four times on a paper in backpocket, the walking
barefooted, sidewalk sunheated.

Second hand book store, Franklin Street, dark green
cover, gilted edges, Walter Pater, roach eaten. A widow
with a magnifying glass examining a postage stamp
with the embossed face of a Sardinian king. A man in beret,
black scarf around wizened neck, searches for shaven nudes,
full page, in Cuban magazines. The empty cot of the owner,
killed by a rat's bite.

The whore sits on the top of the worn marble stairs,
Fortune Street, only her legs visible. Her customers,
conventional minded schoolboys, seventh through the twelfth
grades, from red brick school with the roof that leaks
and molds books. The boys' summum bonum: sneaking a
    smoke
in alleys before classes. Her prices, a dollar a time, two
dollars all night.

TRESTLE

The sky cut apart by black iron,
iron crossing into x's, iron black bolted.
I return in mind
to roam among the wild beans
where I roamed
like a lost dog, sniffing the bushes,
seeking to find where I belonged.
The smell of dog fennel and chinaberry
are still with me. I can
still see on my skin, the color
of the goldenrod that rubbed off on
my arms. I remember tired men
swinging large hammers to drive
spikes into the crossties. I
can still taste the cold water
in the tin cups held to their lips.
First the distance was smoke,
and then an engine, freight cars
carrying cattle to slaughterhouses.
I still have the sad mooing
inside my blood, a sound
pumped through my heart many times,
but never purified, never cleansed.
I remember a man in a blue striped cap
waving, as if he were unaware of his cargo.
He thought I would be routine and friendly.
I spit.
Over all these years, nothing has changed.

POST OFFICE

Clizia, today
I received a letter,
from a professor
in Vienna
with a grant
to study
Klimt and Schiele.
He mentioned
it was snowing,
then hurried
to discuss
a strip teaser,
an American black woman
stepping out
of a white dress,
twenty feet long.

I visualized snowflakes
falling on the shoulders
of the gigantic Goethe,
the grime smeared marble
turning white,
putting a gigantic white lump
in a white park.
I began to feel
excessively melancholy
as I remembered the summer
we watched the bird hop
in the flowers
bedded before the statue.
I thought about
this grey, rose tinted bird
shivering now in the cold.

When at the post office
an old man greeted me.

I looked at his twisted,
puffed, time ruined face,
and wondered who he was.
He told me
we both attended the same college,
were the same age.
He asked what I am doing now,
but I avoided answering.
He talked
about old times,
the day he, Frank, and I
went to a Greek wedding
at Tarpon Springs
and had, as he expressed it,
"a helluva of time".

He interjected that
Frank was still alive,
but crippled by a stroke.
Frank the school wit
could no longer speak.
I could not remember
who Frank was, but recalled
a vague feeling of unrest,
of being out of place
at a public ritual,
this Greek wedding.
I have always been solitary.
Whoever the old man was,
he scribbled on the back
of an envelope
containing an advertisement
about medicare supplements
his address.

Clizia, I returned
to my upstairs, curtained room.
Fumes arose from the wine,
Brunello, a gift
from an expert on Shakespeare.
Framed by the rim of the glass
a tremor of lights,
I gazed and contemplated
the mysteries of these colored specks.

I finally recalled the old man
when he was young,
when he was the same age
as you were
when we were in Vienna,
a few summers ago
when no snowflakes fell
on the shoulders of Goethe.

WHITE TREE BY THE GULF

My life is lived by
a white, barkless shoreline tree
that stands with a dark hole
for a bright woodpecker beside the gulf.
I have stood in the distance
where mangroves arch over
the horseshoe crabs' backs
to watch the rainbowed foam
flow over the white roots.
The distant foam flows inside my body,
its salt, my heart's blood,
the woodpecker's peck, my heart beat.

LUDWIG II

The embroidery:
        thick threads that glitter
ivory and silver swans,
              fleur-de-lys, on a ground
of blue, a curtain
        wrinkled into a variety
of shades: cerulean, turquoise, azure.
              He mused:
what was made
for his private, personal delectation
had through its pomposity
brought reverence from the poor.
                Always
enraptured by textures,
            the touch of skin,
or a sight of the hide of animals,
              he had
ordered his painters to stress the tactile
and
   he ordered the cessation of hunting
at his hunting lodges.
             The wind-swept fur
of the wild rabbit,
        its gyrations, its undulations,
was as sensual,
        as stimulating,
                as exhilarating
as the luxuriant, unrestrained hair
of the Venus in Breling's grotto.
              The wild rabbit
and his provocations of lust
            must be saved
from the puritanical, epicene, asexual
hunters
and their censorship of blood.

                    Outside the snow
fell
      whitening the balustrade,
covering the hedges' leafless stems,
sending out blue shadows
between the thin-trunked trees planted in rows.
                    The nude stone girls
on the stairways
               had white streaks on their contours.
               Alone in a theatre of
his own, only one candle among the many
candles on the candelabra lit, muting
the glow
of the gold leaves
that framed the mirror,
               he waited
for the selections from Tannhauser
to be sung,
       although tonight there would be
no singing.
         In his dining room, the dull
people of his world, the statesmen, the politicians,
the businessmen
            were arguing political theories:
each argument designed
with one purpose in mind:
               how one can get
                    the property of another.
He listens in his mind to Tannhauser telling
Wolfram
       that when Wolfram sings of love
       he sings of what he has never known.
Wolfram's praise of love comes from a cold
and timid heart.
            This praise of love is popular

because it comes from a man
            of feeble emotions
and not an ardent one
who has lived in Venusberg.
                Ludwig feels
paralyzed,
he cannot get up and go to the state dinner,
although
he has arranged for a large bowl of marigolds
to be set in front of him
so he cannot see the others, and others cannot see
him.
    Also, he arranged to have music
played loud,
so he could not hear the petty conversations
around him.
        He will stay all night in the room
and watch
        the candlelight flicker
                    around
the edges of a porcelain carnation.
Meanwhile,
        the men of feeble emotions
meet in the vestibule,
            plot his downfall,
with brides, with lies, with teachery
and prepare
a certification of Ludwig's insanity.

WINTER

Birds, drab brown, pecked on
the snow-covered thatched roof,
as if the winter roof
still had summer seeds.
Out by the grey water, behind
the walls built to defend
the city, although it was
never in danger, burn fires.
From up here on the hill,
the redness in the crenellations
looks like the firing of cannons.
But the mind is shaped
by its own starvation. An invasion
would enliven the quiet
atmosphere. At the small house
by the wagon, the hubs
and rims of its wheels
covered with a thin patina
of yellowed snow, an old
woman, wrapped in two coats,
both cast off by soldiers, leans
on a log fence, and with a small
shovel, its edges bent back and rusty,
looking like the discolored lips
of a man who has drunk
too much sherry, she scrapes
the hard frozen snow, as if
loosening the dirt around the roots
of summer vegetables. Her hands
are gloved in leather, said to have come
from the side of a horse
she used to ride to school
when she was a young girl.

I, now in an upstairs room
above a faceless clock and a sign

with a white unicorn
with a golden horn that swings
on one hook from a chain,
will chime at nightfall, a time
when I will not be noticed.
I will pick up my crutches
and go to another town.

AN EDWARDIAN LADY

You came
all the way
from Torquay
to ask me
about the stranger
who came that day
when the leaves
of the horse chestnut
were starting to curl
and their edges
turn
a brown red.

Have
you
ever seen the inside
of a horse chestnut seed?

It is a
horrible red thing,
veined,
like the head of a
fetus
before it is born.

You would almost
believe
it has an umbilical cord.

Thanks for the stones
you brought
from Torquay.
Each
is a different color,
a different shape.
I love to rub my fingers
around their contours.

I remember him vividly.

The day I saw
his dented dark hat
above the oats,
I heard
the skylark sing
for the first time that year.
The skylark,
a bird that behaves
exactly as Shelley describes,
Shelley,
the most realistic of men.

I have never been
to Torquay,
but I have heard
Torquay has hotels
with pipes to warm
the towels with which
you dry yourself
after a bath.
There is a cliff
which you can climb
and find the chaffinch.
No,
I have
never
been anywhere,
except one trip to Florence
with my father.
I was bored by all those Santa Croce tombs.
Left the others,
sat for hours in the Pazzi Chapel.
The blues of Luca Della Robbia
are the blues
of a song thrush egg.

When I saw this strange man
you asked about,
I was out that day

with my
watercolors,
painting
mistletoe,
the irregularity
of the stems
fascinated me.
I also painted
the yellow crowfoot.
I spent hours
matching my colors
with the colors of the flowers,
but the flowers died, my colors faded.
My colors
now
have
no correspondences
to the original,
but what else is
there for a young girl to do.

But I love to go outside
watch
the sparrows
climb the leaning oats.
When I paint
I raise
this long, stiff,
thick clothed
dress,
let my knees rub the grass,
let the rubbing
redden my skin.
Sometimes I fall into the arms
of the grass
and watch the green hills
roll
with the whiteness of sheep.

When I saw the strange man that day,
his face
was spotted by the shadows
made by the fruit
of the elderberry tree.
He had an agonized look,
a look
I have seen only once before.
in a painting by Pontormo.
My parents shopped on the Ponte Vecchio,
I slipped away
to a small church called Santa Felicita,
there I saw the most agonized face
I had ever seen
until I saw his.

You ask me if we spoke.
No, we
never spoke.
Why are you taking notes?

He is a famous composer, a famous pianist.
But now is in an insane asylum,
his right hand balled into a fist and paralyzed.
He does nothing
but mumble incoherently.

I am sorry.

The day
I saw him,
I observed him
carefully,
scrutinized his every gesture,
his tense fingers pressed on the keyboard of the air.
I do not see
many people.

When he came
near
I remember a
butterfly called the golden white
was hovering over
a marsh marigold in the pond.
My knees pressed
so hard
against the earth
they pained.

He stopped, stared, turned,
went away
to walk among the sheep.
I saw
him touch one sheep
a long, lingering stroke.
You ask me
what is that
by my shoe.
I thought you
came to ask
about him.

It is a hazel nut catkin. Came
out early
due to a mild winter.

The stranger disappeared into
those distant trees.
Once beneath
one of those trees
I found a pile of dead leaves.
When I dug the dead away,
I found
something wild,
but tightly bound,
it had white skin.

LIFE IMITATES ART

My adolescence spent
in museums, regarding
the art
that life will imitate.

A Chinese vase:
the color of a bruise, or a royal
coat sleeve,
or dried blood on the deck of an obsolete battleship,
or the night sky
seen through the swirls
of a closed garden gate,
the garden wall replete
with Spanish tracery—
broken bottles in a border of cement,
and inside, guitar music, castanets, but
outside
an old angel, grey-haired,
with a flaming sword.

A Scriptorium: writing was Writ,
a rectangle printed
on the upper right hand ricepaper corner,
a page
that contained
a miscellany of hermetic expressions—
periphrases,
emblematic images, neologisms, circumlocutions
to seal off meaning
from the uninitiated,
the neophyte, the tyro.
A scribe with bare feet
dips a golden quill
into the golden ink
of a golden inkwell.
Behind his pointed beard, wide eyes,
a nimbus.

His shoulder cloth a gunmetal grey,
highlighted lotus flower blue,
and his shoulder awaits
to be the perch
of a golden bird flying
on a golden background.

The Paradise Garden, painting
by an upper Rhenish master,
early fifteenth century.
A background of a dark ultramarine
sky, cloudless, flat.
On crenelations, bright birds
hop, cling, hang, and peck—
thus natural beings respond
and provide decoration
for a feudal system.
A girl, long hair, reddish, glowing, secured
by emeralds, rubies, pearls
and unclassified jewels,
reads a red covered book, a tale
allegorizing through detailed descriptions
of lust the maintenance of virtue and truth,
ideals designed for the upper classes
who have no social or financial problems.
On a marble table, chiseled
by craftsman to perfection,
five cerise apples, shadowed dark crimson.
Four apples in a bowl, one outside,
peeled, peeling in a curl—
a sinuous triumph of precise paring.
On lush grasses, poppy and daisy sprinkled,
spread out dead, legs upright and stiff,
a dragon, shot by a state supported arrow,
the dragon's face, a human countenance,
the face of the rebellious, poorer classes.

THE CAMERA DI PSICHE,
PALAZZO DEL TE, MANTOVA

The frescoes based on Apuleius
depict
    mankind's
        highest state.
The apex of his
        development
when fused
    with a goat, a horse, a fish
or some other animal existence
becoming
    a centaur
    a satyr
    a merman
or some form of life other than human.
        With this
fusion, this amalgamation
with the unfallen,
        the
transformed or transfigured
human being
    overcomes
    what he lost
    through
        disobedience
in the Garden of Eden.
        Guillio Romano
    and his assistants,
including Primaticcio,
        inculcate
that by not
standing on
    one swollen foot
in a desert
    to subdue
what is animal among the twisted vines

of the soul's jungles,
              but by
leaping
     like a kangaroo, a gazelle,
or duiker
        will the middle link
of being's chain
           ever move up
past the pure intelligences called
angels.

ELEONORA OF TOLEDO

The man with a broad bare back sits on a white horse
pushes
    a purple turbaned old man into the water.
                      A camel
is pulled on shore towards a green rock. Moses
is crossing
      the Red Sea
             on the walls in the room
of Eleonora.

Bronzino has painted her once more in her white,
black,
   glistening brocaded gown,
                   Giovanni, pale,
dying,
   stood by her side.

Giovanni took the goldfinch out of the cage, ran
between the busts of his ancestors and Roman emperors,
held the goldfinch up to the rainbow-colored light
coming through the window's lead circles,
opened to let the bird fly towards the Arno.
Cosimo is always at San Marco, spread out on a straw
mat
in a cell, contemplating the blood that pours
from Jesus' pierced side
           as frescoed by
Fra Angelico.

Although the floor is too thick to hear below
Eleonora knows
     Cosimo's mother
       has urinated
         on the unicorn's horn
in the center of the rug.

Yesterday, after an assassination attempt,
Guiliano Buonnaccorsi

   had the loose skin
   of his aged neck
   pulled tight
   with pincers red hot
and then was dragged by his ankles past the gaze
of the white marble neptune
     of the Ammanati fountain.

After picking up a piece
of broken, salted fish
whose rancid odor oozed on her fingertips
Eleonora
was perplexed
as to where she could wipe her hands
in a room
where all the chairs were covered with crimson velvet
and all the walls
padded with silk,
embroidered with fragile butterflies and delicate trees.

EDICT OF MILAN, CIRCA 300 AD

No, I am not going back to Mediolanum.
It is not the memories: the torture chambers,
but I saw a bishop who wore red gloves
and silver shoes as he stepped on marble,
a girl in a tight fitting green dress,
who sat on a silk cushion and touched
the pearls, the rubies on the covers
of the holy book. Our cause is now fashionable.

I am out in a field near Pavia,
a field that ends in a flat body of water,
a rice paddy. Sheep are herded down to drink,
a crow with a blue body and black wings
flies over. My house is poles propped together,
I eat anything I can find growing on trees, in ground.
I have just eaten a shrivelled green thing,
bitter, my mouth draws. Even if I starve,
I refuse to eat the flesh of an animal.

If this writing seems shaky, it is because
I write with my left hand. My right hand
was cut off at the wrist before the Edict
allowed Christians freedom of worship. It
is difficult to make a legible mark. I
steady my shaking left with the stub of the right.
I write to tell you of the day the Emperor came
from his Golden House to sign the document
that would unchain Christians from the rats.
Constantine kneeled and kissed the eye socket
of one who had had his eye gouged out.

I was present in the cell when the thumbs
broke through the membrane to smash the eyeball.

I heard the screams, watched the executioners' amused faces.
It was at that moment I no longer believed
in a god, omnipotent, omnipresent, omniscient.

Although I no longer believe, do not have any faith,
I took a twig in the shape of a cross,
stuck it in the corner where light comes through a crack.
I look at the twig, the light being caught
where the bark peels off, and then I look
at the empty space at the end of my wrist,
and feel deeply the emptiness.

VIENNA WOODS, 1903

We sit in a terrain that defies,
disconnects all the dictums,
placid and platitudinous, that defend
common sense, reason, transparent language.
These trees have such thick trunks,
stand so close, they create a darkness.
But you Gustav are more
attracted to the darkness than its source,
reverse the traditional
separation of substance from appearance,
disembodying midnight
from the interlinking and entwinement of leaves,
vines, and twigs, and making midnight substantial
without a subject who can misconstrue and imagine time.
You are disappointed because your hand
rubs over roughness, reddens from a surface, bark,
rather than sliding over something that cannot be touched.
You who took the Nike
off the upturned palm of Pallas Athena,
replaced with a girl, modeled by Wally Neuzil
pubic hairs, flaming red, lost the flesh
in the wisdom of the fire.
Your eyes turn towards the light streaks,
the fragmented glints, ovular and floral,
ornament the distance, become incorporeal, sensual flowers
that will send you, Gustav, as it sent Yeats
who discovered sensuality too late, needing
an antidote for insight, to Ravenna
to look at arrested sensuousness
stripped from its source and observed
obtuse, divested of its religious content:
spatial patters glowing out of spandrels,
green, gold acanthus tendrils impervious to winter.
Your birds will eschew flight
to become emeralds and glitter.

Gustav, at this present moment, this unknown
segment of time, at your back a beetle,
a glow, a black rainbow, crawls obscure on dark wood.
I must say, say strongly, the crawl and glow
of this beetle thrills me more
than last evening's performance *al fresco*
of Oscar Wilde's *Birthday of the Infanta*,
acted to be authentic in costumes copied
from the paintings of Velasquez.
The door to your *innenraum*
is locked by your struggle with society,
you the victor became their victim,
as you attack the enemy with weapons
they recognize and know.

You will stand at San Vitale
admiring natural light arranged to dematerialize solidity,
turning surroundings into an illusion.
You will disregard the accumulation of spider webs
nearby in anther dome where lights glitter
as a miracle beyond man's making.
You will come back to Vienna
to paint for the refined and vaporous *haut monde*,
yell, "Ich will loskommen,"
abandon sexual exploration for oblique symbolic statement.
Your watergirls who abandoned their bodies
to the paralyzed flow of stylized water,
subaqueous undulations unknown to octopus and squid,
will become erotic artifice, abstractions liberated from
emotions.

Now you Gustav sit here in the Vienna woods
on a blanket spring spangled with thread flowers,
touch cloth, not the terrifying vegetation, not earth,
the living Cassandra, the living Laocoön,
look as if you were the old man

in your painting *Jurisprudence*, your helpless hands,
arthritic, gripped in cowardice behind your bent back,
your stomach bulges as if pregnant,
your head falls forward as if useless,
you are enclosed, as imprisoned
as your defeated old man
in the womb of a ragdoll, unreal whale.
Your shoulder blades protrude, flap feebly
as if they aspired to be angel's wings and failed.
Soon, you will paint rectilinear geometric forms,
Margaret Stonborough Wittenstein
in a white shimmering dress,
create gardens of flat abstractness.
I have spoken to a dead man for the last time.

A COMPOSER FOR PREPARED PIANO WRITES TO A REPRESENTATIONAL PAINTER

Santa Margherita, Liguria
August 8, 1960

Dear Harry:

The darkness departs to leave
another darkness, the mountain.
Last evening, I walked around
the almost empty docks, listened
to the movement of the masts,
the flapping of the nets,
and a leaf that blew across the beach.
I heard these sounds for the first time,
although I have walked here
everyday for over three months.
Before, I was trying to translate
sounds into the medium of music.
You remember *My Impressions of Italy*.
I destroyed it, for it
was destroying my closeness to Italy.
Now I am truly inspired,
really rapturous for the first time
since I have ceased
composing in the traditional manner.
I now sit in a white room,
my walls are blank, nothing but whiteness,
composing a new work for prepared piano.
It is not the sound I seek,
but the sound before the alteration.
Direction has blunted perception;
what is familiar must be doctored
before it can be heard and become actual.
The only time at a concert
I have ever witnessed an experience of life
was at Woodstock, August 1952,
when John Cage's 4′ 33″ was played,

a complete silence that created nature.
For the first time, the listeners
realized there was an earth.
People became acutely aware
of the sound the wind makes
when it touches leaves, of bird songs,
and the anti-earth, the earth's enemy,
was brought into their awareness
when they heard the harsh sounds
from the highways and others' conversations.

Now if Chopin, Beethoven, Schumann were played,
everyone would have returned
to the blindness and deafness of their egos.
Silence was God creating the earth.
The silence freed people from their self-imprisonment,
encouraged an empathy with their surrounding.
With a new art, the prepared piano,
I might transform people and create a decent society.
You must change your style of painting,
it is immoral to paint traditionally.
I love the earth too much
to continue to compose
according to the tradition of the old,
and you love the earth too much
to continue to paint representationally.

AN EMPLOYEE OF THE
BUREAU OF GERONTOLOGY

An old woman
in her dotage
       sat in the
gable
   of the last gabled house
left
after the demolition project
to beautify
the city
with cubes of cement blocks
covered with pastel paints.

She moved forward
in a continuum,
        as if she were a crewman
        rowing in a shell
        during a regatta,
and then she twisted
her body in undulations,
      as if
a subaqueous sea creature,
one of those sensuous girls
          abandoned
to carnality
    in Klimt's painting,
"Watersnakes II."

      She looked
through a diamond shaped window
of stained glass.
        She bent over
to peer
through a yellow panel,
       and then
       a blue, a red
       a green.

I was
sent out
by the bureau of gerontology
            to write
in the proper space
the problems
        of the old.
I started asking her
all the standard questions.
            She looked at me
            and said,

if you look through the yellow pane
    the sky becomes green grass,
    the grass of a golf course,
    weedless
    and full of holes, and the clouds
become autumn maples
        as seen
in magazines
        advertising trips to the
Smoky Mountains.
            Now, if you look through
the blue,
    the young leaves on the trees
look like
a bruise
under the eye after your son hit you
because
you would not sign your savings to him.
Now, through the green one
the dog run over in the street
looks like
a child wearing an animal mask
and kicking up his rickety legs
as in painting by Max Beckman.

I asked,
    Do you know
art? In college I had a course
on art appreciation.
    She replied,
are you not from Aix-en-Provence
and plan
    to have a dialogue
with a mountain.
        You will
start,
    lonely and isolated,
as you watch the distant mountain,
the mountain
that seems monochrome,
    until
you make the mountain intimate,
bringing it close
    with your brush
to speak varied colors
out of its inwardness.

    Your canvas
will become
    a metaphoric
continuum
between mountain and man.
    The
mountain will caress you
with its warmth,
    and you
will be one of the few men
who ever
had a companion.

I repeated that I was
from the Bureau of Gerontology
and had come
to ask her some questions.

Oh, she said, I thought
you were
Paul Cézanne.

I told her that Cézanne,
according to my memory of the art course,
died long ago,
we were in the United States,
not France.
Paul, she said, you will
learn
we are no where. No where.

I emphasized that I was from
the Bureau of Gerontology.
You are not Cézanne!
she screamed.
You must be a Cubist.
You
have
come
here
to kill me,
to analyze me
into planes.

She began to scream louder.

I ran out
and decided to fake the report.

THE DWARF

The only sky I have ever known
is elongated rectangles of blue,
a distance dissected by bars.
My iron collar, the metal beaten
into crude shapes that resemble roses, chaffs.
I am the queen's entertainment,
her conversation piece.

When unlocked, I am dressed as a shepherdess.
I wear a pink bonnet and carry a ribboned staff.
After being preceded by two trumpeters,
I on a golden horse am pulled by lackeys
before those who control the earth and their priests.

My father never called me "daughter," only "that dwarf."
My mother makes up stories about my size at birth.
Although of normal weight, she lies that I was pea sized.
I brought a high price,
my father bought
a silver statue of a Madonna
who was slender and had high breasts.

God made many mistakes.

WITH BYRON AT DIODATI

Ammerson had brought
        his sketches
of miniatures with Manichean iconography
to show to Claire.
        He said: note the bema
is brushed on with a Chinese stroke. See
the press and the lift, the push and the pull,
the turn and the twist, the dash and the sweep.
A fanned out bristle
and the light touch of the tip.
        Byron was trying
        to tell again
        the story heard
        and heard
about Thriza who when he refused to marry ran out
and stuffed her mouth with grass
        until she suffocated.
When the breath left her body a blue bird
stood on her back.
        Dr. Polidori, fingering
a phial of poison deep in the packet of his
white silk dressing gown, embroidered with
a sunburst
wrote in his journal:
"When we departed Byron waved his
gold-trimmed travelling cap to Hobhouse.
...Byron, the strong swimmer,
the expert sharpshooter, who wrote a poem
that sold fourteen thousand copies in one day,
is totally insensitive to the visual arts."

        Upstairs
Shelley looked at Mary's nudity and screamed
that her breasts
        had eyes instead of nipples.

His candle went immediately out
                         as he ran frantically
towards the forest.

AN UMBRELLA LEAF

High up, supposedly 4,000 feet by
human approximate measurement, I find
a *Diphyllia cymosa*, better known
as umbrella leaf. Its large leaves,
capacious, spread to shelter insects
from moody rains. Concealed in crepuscular
milieux, its miniscule white flowers ascend
above leaves and crisscross with shadows,
mobile in the wind. These specks of whiteness,
greyed a bluish tone, as the shadows
of the folds in the white gown of the girl
surrounded with aureole in Rossetti's
Ecce Ancilla Domini, but sometimes darkened
to resemble Mephistophelian forces
inspiring the emptying of flagons in German taverns
and singing praises to *Le Veau d'Or*.
This plant has no relatives on the mountainside,
but has a cousin in Japan with whom
on holidays it communicates by chthonian telephone.

AN ABANDONED WAREHOUSE
AT CEDAR KEY

I am attracted to abandoned things:
old mistresses discarded by rich lovers,
sick mothers discarded by pampered children,
I have a penchant for the tragic:
crushed cups crowded into garbage cans,
old beer cans with bent sides,
or mattresses thrown among weeds in vacant lots.
I am deeply moved by what has been used
for pleasure and then thrown away.
I never read newspapers unless
they have been bleached blank by the sun.
I go to Cedar Key to walk
through dog fennels by snake shook grasses,
bend under palmettos
to contemplate the rust spots
on the collapsed tin roof of an old warehouse
once used for storing shrimp in wicker baskets.
I am entranced as a saint having a vision
when I see useless gears and pulleys.
I think Tennyson would have been a better poet,
if he had stuck to rusted nails,
fallen rose leaves, shattered spars,
and forgot about the Holy Grail.

VENUS AND ADONIS

On sand where never is a winter freeze,
I glide among sea gulls that squat, stay still,
all one direction pointed, ruffled by breeze,
all tranquil, composed, resigned, reconciled.
Twilight, difficult to separate dark
from light, discern the direction of footmarks.

On motel porch, old man sits, reads the sand;
an old woman recovers from her wounds,
a mugging at Penn Station, near newsstand.
She dreams about youth, tangos, honeymoons;
descants to bring back to life a dead man.
On the beach of the old, darkening sand.

The rare young, Venus and Adonis, stalk
the myths of life, their mirages of delights.
Caught in Cartesian nets, they talk, they walk,
body, soul separate; lies vital, trite.
They see the old as nightmares, ghosts,
reminders of Dictator Death's holocaust.

A spotlight on sea oats' sparrows. In blare
of light, they are sleeping, touching, I have
returned to my room and vin-ordinaire
from a grotesque walk to delay my grave.
In winter, window opened, never cold
on this Florida gulf beach of the old.

VENUS

Leaning against a wall
in a Roman atelier,
she does not arise
on a shell among roses.

She goes unsold,
leaning on a wall
in a Roman atelier.

The young boys grip
the poster
of the strip teaser,
press it next to their hearts,
dance frantically
on the streets
and in the alleys.
She gathers dust,
propped against a wall
in a Roman atelier.

No sea foam scuds
across her heels,
forgotten in an atelier
on a street of whores
in a crowded part of Rome.

THE REPAIRED VENUS

The rim around the dry pool chipped,
fragments, loose, stay in place,
dark gaps wrinkle the curved surface,
Venus, twisting, arises from a shell,

blackened, browned, sun struck.
Her hair ordered to swirls by a hairpin,
her arm distorted, patched by asphalt,
black bracelet around upper arm.

The repaired Venus lifts a foot,
slender, dappled by leaf shadows,
once waterdrops dripped from her toes.

A golden dragonfly, gold net wings
sprinkle her ankle, his scintillations
gold crossing the gap, once anklebone.

OUT IN A PASTURE

Out in a pasture, pouring wine into glasses,
comparing the ruby reflection on grasses,
with the ruby coloring of sundews' globes,
we commented on the beauty of the sound *carnivorous*,
and how, remembering Alexander Pope,
the sound did not fit the sense.
We speculated on what sound makes sense of a bird:
pajaro, Vogel, oiseaux, uccèllo.
We settled on the Italian for warblers,
the German for eagles, the French for swallows,
and dismissed the Spanish.
We turned to the sounds for butterflies,
as a butterfly was flying over,
darkening our hands with fluttering shadows:
mariposa, Schmetterling, papillon, farfalla.
All sounds seem appropriate, even the German.
We repeated the sounds for love:
amor, Liebe, amour, amore.
None seemed to fit, not even English.

THE END OF SOMETHING

We decided that the Marxist dialect of our marriage,
or our liaison or our shacking up
         remained
captive to Hegelian concepts and categories.
                Our
magic materialism
         colluded with the magic idealism
embedded as a preconcluded substructure,
         although
magic idealism
was subverted through ridicule and derision
         at sidewalk
cafes scattered throughout shipping centers
for the affluent.
     Our physical had not escaped
       from moribund metaphysics.
      We decided to examine
our corporeality
  to see if when we adapted
the consensual system of belief
of the truly and only educated,
those with Master's degrees and above in the Humanities,
especially those with degrees
in interdisciplinary endeavors
that combine a study of art, music, literature, philosophy,
psychology and religion,
         those who mix
their Buddhism with Jean Baurillard and Eric Fischl
with a sensitivity attuned
to the Archangel Michael
         as displayed on a Byzantine
book cover of the eleventh century,
         did we
upon adaption to these agreed-upon beliefs and ethics
of the present elite
         only come up
with problematical answers to misconceived questions
and

   really did not have any privileged access
to physical pleasures
               in spite of our unorthodox sexualities.
If you remember,
      we thought when we moved in together
we had transcended the old antinomies,
               but our examination
of our coition
       made us doubt its objective reality
and we found ourselves transcendental idealists.

The result was a loss of prestige
               on both our parts
since we recognized our most lauded value
was only a pointless activity.
               We were confronted
by facing we had followed a flawed axiology.
Our copulations
       were only the old, deluded seeking
of absolute truth.
          Since we cannot live by the illusion
of productive exchange,
           and since your grant was not
renewed
     and you will have no income
             from your study
attempting to show
        that "The Gospel of Thomas"
was prefiguration of Derrida,
           you must remove your
things from the apartment.
            Do not forget that
the Tibetan prayer rug
hanging on the door is really mine,
for I suggested the number
           that resulted in your
winning it in a raffle.

FENCES

This morning, I'm
up early examining
the coloration age
added to fences,
raw cypress, blond,
smears of grey
that wanted
to be green, but failed.
In the Tampa slums,
I live in a fortress
surrounded by a moat,
but I do not have any serfs
to do the unpleasant work,
or captured pagan
to carry out each morning
the garbage.
This one smear
is turning golden,
and looks like a staircase
crowded with women
and painted by Burne-Jones.
All the women
are prim and languid
I think of men
obsessed by their sisters,
Trakl, Khnopff,
and regret I was an only child,
as I stoop down
to pick up an empty bottle
in a brown sack.

A RETURN TO THE 'EIGHTIES

In our, your wife and myself, revolt against illusion,
we failed to recognize
the variability in our actual performance;
for we had substituted a printed text,
a liberating
manual, replenished with illustrations
of acrobatic and oriental sanctioned positions,
for our bodies.

Our learning became so intense and reinforced
that it became a phantasmagoria,
an apocalyptic fantasy.

We have outrun our non-regulating principles,
we find ourselves in a stalemate,
a paralysis of pleasure.

We have lost confidence in the competence of rebellion,
au courant sensuality.
We had believed in au courant sensuality
so religiously
that we overlooked possibilities.
Thus in answer to your crying over the telephone
about your wife leaving you
she is now leaving me and returning to you and the old order
of caring for children and being beaten.

A PHILOSOPHER EATING A LOBSTER

Philosophers sending flecks
through the obscure
dine on lobsters,
suck juice from red claws.
The girl who strolls among
the flickering hermeneutic illumination
of the private dining room
and is friendly to textual glosses,
hangs her dress on the antlers
of ideas slain in a forest of symbols,
parades as a simulation of a simulation.
The philosopher busy
with the metaphysics
of white zinfandel and a boiled potato,
requests she crochet
on her dining room nakedness
the winding-sheet of the West.

LOVE IN THE 'EIGHTIES

Although our bodies were connected,
we operated our love by remote control,
pushing parts of the anatomy to change stations,
if our existences
became uninteresting or were reruns,
or did not live up
to the promises of hypothetical situations
based on the premises
gathered from sex manuals
and x-rated movies.

I think what ruined our love
was that we were caught
in the obsolescence of obscenity,
or was it our Chinese cooking.
We had no phantasies
we were sinning,
and thus our amusement was limited,
or was it cooking in a Wok
that never worked.

There is no use in any longer
continuing our four times a week,
eight to ten PM copulations,
and I am removing the mirror from the ceiling.

A NEOTERIC, THE NEMESIS

I listen to the Gesualdo gestures
of blackened beauty spread over shadows,
your hair falling over spring meadows
embroidered on silk pillow, quadrature.

The raising, the replication of your knee
revolutionizes monody into polyphony;
A copy, Gold relief, Bale altar, 11th century,
on wall, makes esthetic our adultery.

As Rimbaud, I shutter "au passage des chasses
et des hordes", and your husband's hunting gun,
too coarse, obtuse, for trills, fioritura runs,
but in this dice game he deserves his ambsaces.

REPAINTED FOR QUICK SALE

Repainted for quick sale, a happy Jesus
kissing full on the mouth, Mary Magdalene,
she will be repainted a man named Judas
clutching a bag of silver, for betrayal
for hate is easier to sell than love.
Repainted, St. George throwing marshmallows
to an alligator. The alligator will be repainted
a dragon, St. George given a bloody sword,
for cruelty is easier to sell than love.
Venus, with a German expressionist's garish palette,
will be redone without roses and shell
to be a degraded woman, for degradation
is easier to sell than a symbol of holy sex.

TANAGERS

The odors of oranges fresco the corridors.
Its columns crossed by the quest of stained glass,
its ceiling the caprices of circular gold.

I look at what has vanished from the walls,
know I was a stranger to what has gone,
the arrows quivering in a joyous St. Sebastian.

The white space of plaster renews my enigmas
as I stand in this dim light and dream
about sunsets on the flying swallow's wings.

It is not the empurpled drippings of the resurrection
above the candles on the other end,
but another resurrection, a resurrection within:

the child among blazing tanagers on oak limbs.

JAN VERMEER, THE ARTIST IN HIS STUDIO, VIENNA KUNTSTHISTORISHCHES MUSEUM

Her eyelids closed, she holds a yellow book,
a long stemmed musical brass instrument;
she is the only one who can ever look

upon the painter's face, his abolishment,
as she, dazed, stands before a wrinkled map.
His back turned away from all argument.

The scene partially obscured by lush drapes,
a darkened chair with pinpoints of white light,
the painter sketches on canvas blue shapes.

Between them, bric a brac—haphazard, bright—
a marble mask, a manuscript—their masks.
He, tense, awaits her eyes opening outright.

She stands in the blue waters, a blue splash,
brightened by light coming through windowpane,
the blue, engulfing cloth, bleached by stained glass,

darkened to oblivion by artist's brain,
the dark side shadowed by artist's body,
as her blue eyes stay closed in tranquil pain.

The canvas in the canvas unfinished,
in this universe without any blemish.

CHINESE YU VESSEL

As an alien, alone,
    I have left Biblical almugs
and their unseen leaves,
    I have left French alouettes
and their unheard songs,
    to be with archaic Chinese bronzes

of the Chang and Chow periods, to
    meditate on their monsters;
a pig's head on a handle, a pig
    with a half moon
on his head, a blend of the distant
    and the near, the sky

and an animal, eyes with answers.
    A stem on the top
is surrounded by walls that become boats
    about to slide down
a waterfall of metal, float on empty space.
    The stem has a herd

of gazelles whose existence ends at the neck,
    their horns, pure intelligences
as are the bodies of Christian angels.
    At the base is a blend
of snake, lizard, bird, and a human eye,
    the only eye, not blind.

A KINGFISHER OVER
A NORTH CAROLINA RIVER

A blue flash through the river's rising mists,
a probability under a belated moon:
a thin slice of white in another blue, vast—
the excavation of concealed, vague graves.

Bird, a blue arrow, a piercing of the blue
to touch the ashes of a hidden blue,
a phoenix other than a flying bird
arises to bedazzle the wind and roses.

What has been burned, returns not to return,
the blue promises the impossible.
The rattle breaks silence into fragments.

What is blue without your unburned face,
that rattle without your unburned blue voice.
Your appearance, the created and creator.

NEW ALTARS

The thirst of ripened life folds into altars
for the worship of the ambiguous glint of flying birds
and their sinuous shadows crossing the cheeks' hollows,
abolished the alien kiss clutching its silver shadows.

No more begging for the baffled coin, the clink of pride;
no more striving for the funereal gravel of the labyrinth
and its paths mingled with fallen eyelashes and delays
among the pedestals empurpled with lipstick's sneer.

Now aided by seaweed and the gift of coral, I stand
on the shore watching lightning streak the prints
of my bare feet that dint the mysteries of sand
and watching the faint lines of the ibis flying home.

THE PEOPLE AND THE TERRORIST

The people went chatting,
crossing Fifth Avenue.
A terrorist flashed a pistol.

The people organized into an oval
truncated where the terrorist stood,
went on chatting.

The terrorist moved to the right,
the people moved to the right.
The terrorist moved to the left,
the people moved to the left.

The terrorist stepped forward,
the people stepped backward,
The terrorist
and the people were dancing.

The people and the terrorist
moved in accord.

MIGRATIONS AND MYTHS

The soul's eyes watch
the migration of geese,
erase outstretched necks,
substitute a myth.

The soul sees angels
humped over with heaviness
of wings, and singing.

The geese are seeking
what man has left
of their ancient landing.

The white around their necks,
neither snow nor ivory,
only white around their necks.

To the soul, the geese
are angels singing
about the undecipherable
in an air with a gold background.

PROCESSION IN PISA

Boys with candles chant canticles,
white robed boys sing about angels.
Sparrows flap brown wings in grey sand.

Boys with candles march toward cemeteries,
intone sad songs counterfeiting sorrows.
Grasshoppers reveal yellow streaked black backs.

Boys with candles chant dirges, daydream
about monsters devouring virgins.
A ladybug uplifts white spotted orange wings.

CONTRASTS

Angels who wear flat cerise gowns
are rising out of catastrophes.

Those who know they do not know
what they desired when desiring
grind the air into lumps of gold.

Angels who wear flat saffron gowns
are rising out of smears and blurs.

Those who know their words are not words
find the true word in the voice
of the ancient tenor singing falsetto.

Angels who wear flat sapphire gowns
are rising from the gourmets' groans.